Visualization

The Unveiled Extraordinarily Simple Procedures To
Materialize Your Aspirations By Harnessing The Potency
Of Creative Visualization

*(Enhancing Your Life And Achieving Mental Clarity
Through Visualization Methods)*

Maurilio Castellanos

TABLE OF CONTENT

Data Mining Tools

As previously stated, data mining employs a repertoire of methodologies incorporating distinct algorithms, statistical analysis, database systems, and artificial intelligence for the purpose of scrutinizing and evaluating data derived from diverse data sources and perspectives. The majority of data mining tools possess the capability to identify a variety of classifications, tendencies, and configurations in extensive sets of data. These tools additionally convert the data into refined information.

Several of these frameworks and techniques facilitate the execution of diverse actions and activities that are crucial for conducting data mining analysis. These data mining tools and techniques allow for the application of various algorithms, such as classification and clustering, on your dataset. The techniques utilized employ a structured framework, offering profound understandings into the data and manifold phenomena that are encapsulated within the dataset. These frameworks are commonly referred to as data mining tools.

This examines several prevalent data mining tools employed within the industry.

Orange Data Mining

Orange is a software application that employs various machine learning and data mining tools. Additionally, it possesses the capability to facilitate data visualization and serves as a software module, specifically constructed using the Python programming language. This application has been developed by the esteemed faculty of information and computer science at Ljubljana University, located in Slovenia. Given that this application relies on components that are based on software, it is appropriate to designate these components as widgets. The various widgets employed within the application serve the purpose of carrying out preprocessing tasks and facilitating data visualization. With the employment of these widgets, you can evaluate diverse algorithms for the purpose of data mining and additionally employ them for predictive modeling. These widgets possess diverse capabilities, such as

Data reading

Presenting data in tabular format

Choosing specific attributes from the dataset

A Comparative Analysis of Diverse Learning Algorithms

Training predictors

Data visualization

Orange also offers an interactive user interface that enhances user experience when utilizing various analytical tools. The applications can be easily navigated.

What are the Benefits of Utilizing Orange?

If one possesses data gathered from various sources, it can be expeditiously formatted and organized within this application. One can reformat the data, adhering to the prescribed pattern, and rearrange the widgets strategically to enhance the interface. Various users can utilize this application, as it enables users to efficiently make intelligent choices in a limited timeframe. This can be accomplished through the examination and comparison of data. Orange is a highly effective means of representing data obtained from open-source platforms. Furthermore, it provides users with the capability to assess various sets of data. Data mining can be conducted by employing various programming languages, such as Python and visual programming. A variety of analyses can be conducted using this platform.

Additionally, the program offers machine learning functionality, text mining capabilities, and supplementary tools tailored for bioinformatics purposes. Additionally, this software incorporates various data analytics functionalities and is accompanied by a python library.

One can execute various Python scripts within a terminal interface or employ an integrated development environment (IDE), such as PythonWin, PyCharm, or interactive shells like iPython. The application features a canvas interface where the widget can be positioned. Thereafter, you have the ability to generate a workflow within the interface in order to analyze the dataset. Additionally, the widget has the capability to execute essential tasks such as displaying a data table, extracting information from the data, training predictive models, identifying relevant features from the dataset, creating visual representations of the data elements, and evaluating the performance of different machine learning algorithms. The software is compatible with a variety of Linux operating systems, Windows, and Mac OS X. Moreover, it is equipped with classification and multiple regression algorithms.

This application is also capable of parsing documents in their original or alternative file formats. It employs distinct machine learning methodologies to categorize and group the data, thereby facilitating the process of supervised data mining. Classification algorithms employ two categories of entities, specifically classifiers and learners. A student is referred to as class-leveled data, and it utilizes the data in order to provide the classifier. In orange, regression methods can be employed as well. These techniques bear resemblance to classification methods in that they are both intended for supervised data mining and rely on class-level data. The conglomerate will persist in acquiring knowledge through the fusion of insights derived from the individual model and meticulous metrics. The model you develop may arise from the utilization of distinct learners or distinct training data on identical data sets.

Learners can be diversified further by modifying the parameter set employed by them. In this particular software, one can generate ensembles by encompassing them around various learners. These ensembles exhibit similar behavior as other learners, but their outputs enable the prediction of results for any given data instance.

SAS Data Mining

The SAS institute has pioneered the development of the Statistical Analysis System (SAS), which is widely employed for the purposes of data management and analytics. SAS can be utilized for data mining, information management from diverse sources, data transformation, and statistical analysis. Non-technical users can also avail themselves of the graphical user interface as a means of interacting with the application. The SAS data miner effectively evaluates expansive data sets, enabling users to derive precise insights that inform optimal decision-making. The SAS platform employs a distributed memory processing architecture that allows for various forms of scalability. This application possesses the capability to facilitate data optimization, extraction, and textual mining.

DataMelt Data Mining

DataMelt, referred to as DMelt, is an advanced visualization and computational platform that provides users with an interactive framework enabling the exploration of data visualization and analysis. This application has been specifically developed for professionals in the field of data science, engineering, and academic individuals. This application employs a cross-platform utility and is implemented using the Java programming language. This application is compatible with various operating systems, provided they are able to support a Java Virtual Machine (JVM). This application comprises libraries for mathematics and science.

Utilization of Mathematical Libraries: The application makes use of various libraries for purposes such as executing algorithms, generating random numbers, and performing curve fitting.

Scientific Libraries: The libraries employed are intended for the rendering of three-dimensional or two-dimensional graphical representations.

DMelt has the capability to facilitate the analysis of vast quantities of data, perform statistical analysis, as well as engage in data mining processes. This application finds utility in the realms of financial markets, engineering, and the natural sciences.

Rattle

This tool or application employs a graphical user interface (GUI) to facilitate user interaction. The Rattle software has been constructed utilizing the R programming language. In addition, the application also showcases the statistical capabilities of R and provides a range of data mining functionalities that can be utilized throughout the mining procedure. Rattle boasts a sophisticated and extensive user interface, which incorporates an integrated log tab that empowers users to generate code for executing diverse graphical user interface (GUI) operations. The application is capable of generating data sets, and provides options to modify and observe them. Furthermore, the application enables users to comprehensively evaluate the code, employ it for diverse objectives, and expand upon the existing code without any limitations.

Rapid Miner
The majority of data mining experts employ the use of rapid miner software in order to carry out predictive analytics.

This particular tool was designed and created by a corporate entity known as Rapid Miner. The code has been implemented using the Javascript programming language, and it provides users with a cohesive platform through which they can execute diverse tasks beyond predictive analysis, including deep learning, machine learning, and text mining. Rapid Miner has versatile applications, spanning diverse areas including commercial enterprises, academic institutions, research facilities, training institutes, machine learning domains, software development, and corporate organizations. Rapid miner also provides users with a server on-site. Furthermore, it provides users with the option to leverage either private or public cloud infrastructure for the purpose of storing the data and conducting operations on said data set. The fundamental structure of this application is predicated upon a client/server model. This application exhibits a considerable degree of accuracy in comparison to alternative applications and tools, owing to its utilization of a template-based framework.

Optimizing Concentration Via The Practice Of Meditation

In the following , we shall delve into three fundamental meditation approaches that can be adopted. There exist numerous variations of these meditation approaches, however, it is imperative that you experiment with each one in order to determine which one is most effective for you. It is essential to bear in mind the underlying purpose for engaging in the practice of meditation. You are not solely engaging in this activity for the significant sense of tranquility and serenity it generates.

As stated earlier in a preceding , meditation has been substantiated through numerous research studies to effectively diminish hypertension, engender significant mental serenity, and alleviate a considerable magnitude of stress. Meditation is effective, however, it does not encompass the specific advantages you seek.

You are seeking a highly specialized advantage derived from the practice of meditation, namely an enhanced capacity for unwavering concentration. This is the key. Hence, the rationale for embracing a meditation practice lies within this context. It is imperative to possess such concentration in order to manifest your personal visions of an alternative reality into an actuality in which you reside. Please be aware of the following.

The essence of meditation

Despite the diversity of meditation practices derived from various philosophical and spiritual traditions globally, they all share a fundamental element in common. Each of these diverse practices exhibits variances in terminology, procedures, and frameworks; nevertheless, when one delves beneath the surface, a fundamental similarity emerges.

The shared characteristic lies in their ability to cultivate your attention towards the current moment. You refrain from harboring prolonged thoughts on prior events. You do not attend to recollections. You do not harbor concerns regarding the future. One refrains from making assumptions or conjectures regarding future occurrences. On the contrary, it is imperative that you redirect your attention to your present state on a continual basis, monitoring every passing moment. The cultivation of a profound tranquility occurs as your ability to concentrate becomes honed, akin to a laser, singularly directed towards a specific moment and location. You persevere in a perpetually timeless state.

Consider your mind as a vast expanse akin to the vastness of the ocean. At the summit, there will be a plethora of theatricality. There will be a substantial amount of stress, concerns, anxieties, and frustrations. However, if one were to descend to a depth of 200 feet, the prevailing conditions would be remarkably tranquil. There is occasional turbulence observed, albeit minimal, as it is situated in a tranquil space isolated from the accompanying commotion on the surface.

If one were to descend to a point close to the ocean floor, situated approximately one foot above it, a state of absolute tranquility would prevail. That is a reflection of the functioning of your cognitive processes. There exists within oneself a tranquil core that facilitates the release of an immense level of concentration. Nevertheless, achieving such a state can only be attained by cultivating mental resilience to transcend the superficial aspects of one's existence, delving beyond the layers of tranquility within oneself, and ultimately reaching the essence at the very center.

There exist three methodologies that can be employed to accomplish this task. Once more, as previously stated, these methodologies encompass a wide range of variations, nevertheless, all existing meditation techniques can essentially be classified into these three fundamental approaches.

Counting your breath

Engaging in the act of observing and tallying your breath serves as a relatively uncomplicated technique for conducting meditation. One could locate a serene chamber and assume a relaxed posture. There is no obligation for you to adopt the lotus position. There is no obligation for you to adopt a posture resembling that of the Buddha. Kindly assume your usual seated position to ensure your comfort. Nevertheless, it is imperative that you do not become excessively at ease to the point where you doze off.

Maintaining an upright posture is of utmost significance, as it ensures that your attention remains directed towards the intended objective. To initiate this exercise, you may commence by gently shutting your eyes and engaging in deliberate, relaxed inhalation and exhalation. You engage in repetition of this action on multiple occasions, subsequently decelerating your respiration further, and solely focusing your awareness on the inhalation and exhalation of air within your body. It is imperative that you employ diaphragmatic breathing. This area corresponds to your abdominal region or the lower portion of your stomach. It is recommended to interlock your fingers or join your hands together, positioning them beneath your navel, and proceeding to inhale into this enclosed space or breathe into your hands. Please proceed with caution, taking your time and directing your attention towards your breathing.

After engaging in this practice for a prolonged duration, one attains a state of tranquility where the sole concentration lies on one's breath. You stop worrying. Ideas no longer manifest to the degree at which you evaluate them, or induce anxiety within you. They simply drift through the recesses of your thoughts akin to ethereal formations. The sole sensory focus of your practice of counting your breath is your breath. This task necessitates being completed across multiple days and weeks.

Furthermore, the gauge of accomplishment lies in the level of concentration one can maintain on their breath, unhindered by any form of diversion. This practice is truly commendable as it leads to the cessation of thought judgment over time. They transform into ephemeral clouds traversing the sky, rendering them trivial. The crucial aspect is your conscious acknowledgement of your breathing pattern, with undivided attention solely devoted to this.

Transcendental meditation

Transcendental meditation and conscious breath counting share many similarities. You undergo an identical procedure akin to tallying your breath. A notable distinction lies in the fact that in the practice of transcendental meditation, one engages in the recitation of a silent mantra. You do not articulate or speak your mantra orally. One does not vocalize or articulate it. There is an absence of vocalization, one does not even utter it-- the state of silence prevails. You say it mentally.

How does this work? You duly "recite" the mantra subsequent to inhaling, and subsequent to exhaling. This technique holds great efficacy as, upon being practiced diligently over multiple intervals spanning several days, your mantra assumes a pivotal role in harmonizing your breath. Gradually, your attention shifts from your breath to your chosen mantra. Your mantra represents the focal point of your attention.

It is crucial to bear in mind that the selected mantra word must consist of only one syllable or one vowel and should carry no semantic meaning. This is really important. It is imperative that the word chosen does not fall under the categories of mom or dad. The utilization of a word elicits cognitive processes. The ultimate objective of transcendental meditation is to eliminate or transcend the mental activity within the mind.

When transcendental meditation is executed correctly, one's concentration becomes so intensely honed in on the mantra that there is scant space for the emergence of thoughts. You are incapable of generating ideas and subsequently evaluating them. One does not have the opportunity to succumb to emotional reactions due to one's discernment. This form of meditation engenders a profound sense of tranquility and serenity, as well as vitality.

It enjoys a considerable global following owing to its inherent simplicity and refined aesthetic. Direct your attention solely to the mantra, as all other concerns will subsequently be attended to. As you cultivate your attention on the mantra, even the rhythm of your breath seamlessly integrates with the panning.

Single object focus

The practice of directing one's attention solely on a singular object is a distinct and dissimilar manifestation of meditation. If one does not possess a genuine inclination towards entering a dimly lit or tranquil and isolated environment, or engaging in meditative practices like breath counting, an alternative approach could involve directing one's focus solely on a single object. You simply require a period of uninterrupted time. This is really important. It is imperative that you allocate a sufficient amount of time for the purpose of engaging in this meditation practice. The only requirement is for you to be seated in a comfortable manner.

Once more, it is not necessary for you to drift into slumber; rather, you merely need to assume an upright posture or adopt a position that deters drowsiness.

Subsequently, you direct your gaze towards an object. It may constitute a volume within your collection of books. It could potentially be a writing instrument situated on the surface of your desk, or alternatively, a tree located in close proximity to your window. The essential aspect is to dedicate the entirety of your meditation period to focused observation of a single object.

When conducting an examination, one shall navigate the outer perimeters or confines of the entity and activate their innate curiosity. It is of utmost importance to emphasize that when you are curious, you are not inquiring. This distinction is pivotal when comparing this form of curiosity to conventional curiosity. In a state of curiosity, one generally tends to inquire with a significant number of queries.

As an instance, suppose you observe a wallet lying on the ground. Without delay, one would inquire as to the individual responsible for misplacing this wallet. Was the wallet inadvertently dropped or misplaced, or does its presence potentially indicate involvement in criminal activity? Numerous inquiries arise in one's mind. That is not the form of curiosity I am referring to.

In contrast, when engaging in solitary object concentration meditation, one's attention resides in a state of profound curiosity regarding the parameters or features of the chosen object. One observes intricacies such as how light interacts with it, its distinct hues, meticulously seeking to unravel a plethora of finer details. You do not have an intention to inquire about the reason. You are simply seeking an increasing amount of information. Throughout the duration of your meditation, you engage in deep focus on a singular object.

This particular method of meditation holds great efficacy as it facilitates the purging of all thoughts, allowing one's creative and focusing abilities to be concentrated solely on a singular object. Moreover, the mind is calmed by the deliberate narrowing of attention to a singular input, thus cultivating a sense of inquiry while facilitating quietude. You do not attend to or address your respiration. One does not employ a mantra. Simply concentrate on an object, and you will discover that this approach effectively induces a significant level of mental relaxation. You achieve a state of mental relaxation when you engage in single object focus.

There is no definitive or erroneous response in regards to your selection among the three meditation strategies elucidated earlier. The cognitive processes of individuals vary greatly. We possess distinct cognitive tendencies and modes, frequently stemming from our diverse life experiences. The crucial aspect lies in discerning the technique that most effectively enhances your concentration and persisting in its practice. This is how you improve your concentration.

It is essential to continually bear in mind that the primary objective of your meditation practice is not solely to attain inner tranquility and serenity, although these advantages can certainly be gained. The fundamental purpose for engaging in meditation is to augment your aptitude for concentration. It will be necessary for the purpose of engaging in creative visualization.

Developing Self-Belief

Self-assurance is acquired gradually. Prioritize developing a sense of ease and familiarity with the way you envision your own self. As an illustration, it is possible that you will discover alternative methods of meditation that align more effectively with your preferences. If you possess the capability to comprehend and adhere to the intricacies of yoga, it is conceivable that the contemplative techniques employed in yoga can potentially facilitate your progress towards a state conducive to effective visualization. Certain individuals find deep meditation to be effective, as it facilitates heightened sensory perception, enabling them to gain greater self-awareness than simply looking at themselves in a mirror.

The internal state of one's emotions holds significant importance. If one does not experience a sense of comfort and inner peace, it is highly probable that such unease would manifest outwardly. It is essential to engage in regular meditation practice as it facilitates a heightened sense of openness and awareness within oneself. It possesses the ability to identify imperfections and rectify them. It possesses the ability to perceive erroneous thought patterns and reframe them in a more insightful manner. It can enhance oxygen circulation throughout the body, inducing a notably increased sense of relaxation beyond an individual's usual level of composure.

Self-assurance emanates from the capacity to mentally picture oneself in various scenarios and exhibit complete composure in each. Witness yourself gracefully move across the dance floor, drawing nearer to him. Visualize yourself positioned on a podium, delivering a speech to an audience of one thousand individuals. Observe as your mouth parts and your words take shape; however, instead of mere muttering, envision them gracefully emanating from your lips and drifting towards the attentive audience, where they shall be earnestly heard. Sensate the air propelling the words, bestowing upon them the resilience and influence indispensable to effectively convey the message. Should you have faith in your capabilities and possess the capacity to envision them beforehand, it will become evident that when the actual circumstance materializes, it effortlessly aligns with your inherent nature, rather than exerting undue pressure on you.

When my hands hit the ivories of the piano, I was a concert pianist. Irrespective of whether I had an audience comprising a sole individual or a gathering of 2000, my internal sensation remained unaltered. I infused each stroke of the keys with sentiment, resulting in an enchanting quality to the music. The notion of the piano serving as an extension of my hands was so deeply embedded in my mind that when it materialized, it posed no challenge for me to execute with excellence. It seemed as though I had perpetually been engaged in that precise activity.

Due to this rationale, engaging in meditative visualization confers a distinct advantage, fostering increased self-assurance across all facets of your existence. It is possible that you encounter challenges in interpersonal communication and find yourself feeling intimidated by others. They may not possess conscious awareness of engaging in this behavior, as the sense of intimidation could potentially originate from within one's own psyche. Once you relinquish the notion of feeling intimidated and instead recognize the profound influence exerted by your own spoken words, this realization will engender a transformative shift in your life, indefinitely.

Modifying your perspective on existence

To effectuate a modification in your approach towards life, it is imperative to ascertain the aspects in which you err. If faced with an area of discomfort, endeavor to identify and comprehend its specific nature and root causes. For example:

I experience profound discomfort when entering enclosed spaces, as I am plagued by the persistent sensation of being under intense scrutiny by those present.

In this case which is quite common with people who have self-esteem issues, the way to teach the mind to see things differently is to take out the element of the audience. It is evident that the individual's primary concern lies with the audience rather than the entrance. Therefore, eliminate the presence of the audience during the act of visualization and solely envision executing a flawless entrance. It is possible that the selected shoes are those that cause instability while walking. It is possible that the attire being worn is not conducive to comfort. It is imperative to gain a comprehensive understanding of the entire scenario and proceed methodically, addressing each element meticulously, in order to attain a flawlessly executed presentation that reintroduces the audience, subsequent to resolving any potential pitfalls.

I experienced a sense of embarrassment as the teacher directed a question toward me, which gave the impression that I was being portrayed in a foolish manner.

In this hypothetical situation, the student experiences a sense of being singled out and is unease with this perception. Nevertheless, if the student possesses the responses and demonstrates swiftness in providing them, the unease becomes unnecessary. The imagery in this instance would enhance affirmative interaction between the instructor and the pupil. Envision a contest of intellect. Envision the remark made by the instructor, succeeded by your own. Envision the harmonious connection, rather than apprehending the potential catastrophe. If you are able to conjure a conception of communicative concord between yourself and another party, you may discover that this absence of harmony was the principal lacking element from the outset. The teacher held no preconceived notions regarding your capabilities, and despite your apprehension, there was hardly any basis for such apprehension. Your responses to inquiries would likely exhibit the same level of insightful analysis as those of your fellow classmates.

The practice of visualization enables individuals to perceive the true essence of a given circumstance and mentally experience it in advance of its occurrence. By adopting such an approach, you ensure that you are adequately equipped to face any unfortunate circumstances that may arise. It is a rare occurrence for individuals who do not possess inherent expectations. Therefore, by engaging in such visualizations, you enhance both your self-assurance and your aptitude for social interaction. In your mental imagery, you transcend your initial timid and introverted nature to embody a persona that effortlessly engages with others. This mirrors my own experience of envisioning myself confidently playing the piano before a live audience.

By altering one's perspective on life, one can experience personal benefits as it eliminates the sense of helplessness in any given circumstance. Envision it; visualize it with your mental faculties, simulate the scenario, and thus equip yourself for its eventual occurrence. Undoubtedly, errors are bound to occur, yet they stem from our nature as humans, unrelated to any potential concerns about self-worth that you might have. You can enhance your experiences by proactively envisioning scenarios and rehearsing them beforehand, thereby ensuring that you are always prepared and avoid any unexpected situations.

Are You Desirous Of Attaining Your Objectives?

A common attribute shared by all individuals is their aspiration for achievement. We collectively share the aspiration of attaining a level of success that grants us the means to live a comfortable life as we have long imagined - the ability to acquire desired possessions, reside in an exquisite abode alongside our loved ones, or even establish a thriving enterprise of our own. Despite the optimism it may present, the path to achieving success is fraught with challenges and obstacles. It is an arduous and rugged path that ultimately guides you to a destination for leisure. It's worth the wait.

Procedures on the Pathway to Achieving Success

Attaining your objectives may present challenges along the way, however, the difficulty level can escalate significantly if you fail to establish a clear direction and lack the necessary resources to propel yourself towards the ultimate success. Fortunately, success is attainable for all, including yourself. Simply have faith and successfully manifest your desires.

Dream big. Do not hesitate to envision aspirations that appear beyond reach, as your present circumstances do not dictate your future. Push yourself to rise above your limitations and break free from the confines of your comfort zone by embracing challenges and setting lofty aspirations. The grander your aspirations, the greater your drive and enthusiasm shall be, leading you to embrace fresh trials and prospects with an open mind.

Believe in your dreams. You must possess the determination to bring them into fruition. If you do not have faith in your visions, no one else will. Formulate the dreams or aspirations you wish to actualize, visualize the desired life you seek, and steadfastly have faith in it. Develop a mentality geared towards success that empowers you to effectively navigate and overcome various obstacles. By adopting this perspective, you will be capable of overcoming setbacks that may otherwise hinder or demotivate you in the pursuit of your objectives. Initiating this process can prove challenging, particularly when one has been accustomed to engaging in complaints or when individuals find themselves amidst an environment that fosters negativity. Approach the situation with a day-by-day mindset and initiate the practice of observing your thoughts.

Surround yourself with individuals who have unwavering faith in your abilities. Eliminate those purported friends who consistently undermine your efforts and assert that your aspirations are unattainable. The former individuals are those who ardently advocate against surrendering one's aspirations, offering support and motivation to persevere in the face of setbacks. Conversely, the latter group consists of individuals whose presence may prove detrimental, making it advisable to refrain from investing one's valuable time and energy. Retain the favorable individuals and release the unfavorable ones. Draw inspiration from individuals within your acquaintanceship who have achieved their aspirations despite facing adversity rooted in a socioeconomically disadvantaged backdrop. These individuals serve as compelling evidence that one can achieve any aspirations they set their mind to, provided they possess unwavering belief and dedication towards their pursuit.

Reflect upon the significant strides you have made in your journey. In situations of despondency or the inclination to abandon one's pursuit, it is essential to recall the considerable progress one has made and the proximity to the achievement of their aspiration. If your perception aligns with the notion that your time and effort have been squandered on a futile undertaking, allow me to correct you. Keep in mind that the path to success does not come without challenges, thus requiring perseverance to overcome obstacles before finally experiencing prosperity. Should you choose to relinquish your pursuit at this juncture, your diligent endeavors will be rendered futile, ultimately dissipating into insignificance. Cultivating a mindset geared towards success yields numerous advantages when it comes to achieving our objectives. Frequently, we hinder our own path towards success due to our mindset characterized by uncertainty, inadequate self-assurance, and a limited resolve to achieve. Our cognitive processes determine our actions. Should we harbor doubts about our capacity to achieve greatness, the realization of our dreams may prove unattainable. Nevertheless, by maintaining an optimistic outlook, you will undoubtedly attain success and fulfill your aspirations. The significance of our mindset in establishing and attaining our goals cannot be overstated.

Discipline is the Key

When establishing your objectives, it is imperative that you demonstrate unwavering dedication towards achieving them. One must strive to unite the aspirations and wishes they hold dear, in a sense, marrying them together. In order to ensure its successful outcome, it is imperative that you willingly surrender yourself to their cause. Self-control is an integral factor in achieving success in one's life. It is imperative to attain a state of equilibrium and concentrate your efforts in order to achieve success. In order to mitigate the pressure associated with achieving your goals, there are specific actions that can be taken to effectively minimize susceptibility to frequent and intense stress.

Manage your time. Make a daily or as-needed record of tasks by jotting down a to-do list, and prioritize them based on their importance and urgency. This will assist you in preventing exhaustion, engaging in last-minute rushes to meet deadlines, or neglecting critical responsibilities that could have made a favorable impression on your employer or higher-ranking individual. Allocate a daily timeframe exclusively for personal pursuits wherein you may engage in activities of your choice, whether it be reading a book, viewing a film, or engaging in physical exercise. An hour or two should suffice.

Assess your progress. Examining the progress you have achieved thus far in your present stage of life will instill the drive to persist and persevere on a daily basis. Reflect on your initial aspirations and endeavors, and juxtapose them with your current state of being. You shall be astonished by the considerable progress you have achieved.

Pursuing one's aspirations is not an imprudent endeavor as long as one possesses a clear sense of purpose. Should we allow ourselves to be consumed by fear and resist embracing change and exploring new opportunities, we will forever find ourselves trapped in a stagnant existence. If one does not exert effort in striving for the realization of their aspirations, those aspirations will perpetually remain unfulfilled. We possess the agency to shape our own future. It is within our purview to determine whether the future is a promising one or a bleak one. The initial stride towards a more promising future commences with your conviction in its attainability. Failure is an inevitable aspect of life from which we cannot exempt ourselves, but it is also transient in nature. Through persistent efforts and unwavering determination, even in the face of repeated setbacks, you will eventually witness the realization of your aspirations. Please persist in your efforts and refrain from surrendering.

What Are Some Uses For Visualization?

Scientific Visualization

It entails the portrayal, curation, and conversion of experimental or simulated data, accompanied by an overt or inferred geometric configuration, aimed at facilitating the exploration, comprehension, and analysis of the data. It prioritizes and accentuates the depiction of advanced level data through the utilization of animation and graphics methodologies.

.

Educational Visualization

It entails employing an unconventional digital recreation to produce an image that can be subjected to classroom discussion or pedagogical instruction. This teaching tool is highly effective and extremely valuable.

Information Visualization
It centers its attention on harnessing computer-supported tools to explore vast amounts of theoretical data. Robust techniques enable users or consumers to concurrently modify the visualization.

Knowledge Visualization
When employing diagrammatic representations as a means of transmitting information between individuals, the objective is to foster the exchange of knowledge through computer-aided visualization, rather than relying solely on non-computerized means.

Product Visualization
Proficiency in visualization software is required in order to effectively examine and manipulate technical drawings, 3D models, and other associated documentation pertaining to artificial machinery and large product assemblies.

Systems Visualization
This can be referred to as the emerging discipline of visualization that encompasses established methodologies

while incorporating techniques of narrative storytelling. It acknowledges the importance of complex systems theory and the interconnectedness of systems, as well as the necessity of knowledge representation.

Visual communication
This diagram represents the expression of viewpoints by means of informational display. This is primarily associated with the 2-dimensional visual representations that encompass electronic resources, alphanumeric characters, and artistic symbols. Recent investigations in this specific domain have focused on the usability of graphics and web design.

Visual analytics
The primary objective of this Analysis is to examine the manner in which individuals engage with visualization methods within the broader context of data analysis. These analytics can be described as the approach to analytical

reasoning that is enhanced by the use of an interactive visual interface.

The primary emphasis lies on the individual's engagement with information and the evolving nature of information spaces. This research focuses on providing assistance for cognitive processes and perceptual abilities that allow users to perceive the anticipated and discover the unexpected within intricate informational contexts.

This document is intended to furnish precise and trustworthy information pertaining to the subject matter and concern addressed. The publication is marketed under the premise that the publisher is not obligated to provide accounting, authorized, or any other type of proficient services. If there is a need for guidance, particularly of a legal or professional nature, it is recommended to engage the services of a knowledgeable individual within the respective field.

- As per a Declaration of Principles which garnered acceptance and approval from an equal participation of the American Bar Association's committee and a committee representing publishers and associations.

The information presented herein is declared to be true and reliable. The recipient reader bears full and sole responsibility for any potential liability resulting from negligence or misuse of the policies, processes, or instructions provided. The publisher shall not be held legally responsible or liable for any compensation, harm, or financial detriment arising from the information provided herein, in any situation whatsoever.

The publisher does not hold the copyrights, instead they are owned by the respective authors.

The information provided herein is intended solely for informational purposes and is universally applicable. The provision of the information is devoid of any contractual or guarantee assurance.

The trademarks utilized are devoid of any form of authorization, and the dissemination of said trademark occurs without the explicit consent or endorsement of the trademark proprietor. The trademarks and brands mentioned in this book serve solely for elucidation and are exclusively owned by their respective owners, without any affiliation to this document.

Installing A Vision Board

When engaging in the process of cultivating affirmations, it is occasionally necessary to be prompted regarding one's perceived identity or justified entitlements. The essential idea is that individuals who do not employ positive affirmation as a means to progress in life do so haphazardly, frequently encountering disillusionment and surrendering control of their lives to the influence of others. A vision board serves as a facilitator to achieve this objective, albeit governed by specific guidelines. For instance, extravagant aspirations such as attaining a million-dollar sum are not appropriate. This underscores the fact that your desired outcome has not yet been achieved and necessitates a shift in mindset. It is crucial for you to behold the achievement and firmly attain it.

Allow me to elucidate this matter in a more concise manner. An affluent individual possesses a distinctive thought process. Upon waking in the morning, his mental focus primarily revolves around his wealth and business endeavors, reflecting the mindset of affluence. An impoverished laborer awakens each morning with the mindset of someone facing financial hardships. Individuals who have aspirations that remain unfulfilled experience a profound sense of disappointment upon waking in the morning, as they are confronted with the realization that their dreams have not been realized. One must align their thinking with the mindset prevailing within the contextual framework of their aspiration. As an instance, if your goal is to attain wealth, it is imperative to adopt the mindset of an affluent individual. To become a seasoned traveler, it is imperative to adopt the mindset of a traveler. You possess immense cognitive ability that remains untapped. Hence, regulations govern the content that is included in your vision board.

• The usage of the present tense is mandatory, and it should be expressed in complete sentences.
• The phrases utilized should possess significance • The expressions employed must hold significance • The phrases utilized need to be meaningful • The utilized phrases must carry significance
- It is expected that you employ specific key terms in your everyday communication.
Therefore, should you aspire to become a concert pianist, expressions such as:

• I possess exceptional piano-playing abilities that few can rival in this county.

I am a highly acclaimed concert pianist who receives overwhelming adoration from audiences.

● I invest my utmost emotional intensity into the piano pieces I perform.

● My piano playing is highly regarded by others.

I employed this particular item due to its familiarity from my childhood, during which time I partook in piano lessons. I aspired to transcend mediocrity, and while engaged in playing the piano, I wholeheartedly held absolute faith in the veracity of the aforementioned assertions. When you mentally envision yourself in this scenario, you perceive the sound of applause. Your cognitive abilities are appropriately aligned, allowing you to transcend the perception of being a mere student. You emanate the aura of immense accomplishment, and it holds utmost significance to genuinely internalize this belief due to its capacity to trigger the release of specific hormones in your body that reinforce this conviction, fostering a winner's mindset. Have you ever experienced a sense of melancholy or unease when the skies appear overcast and the world takes on a somber hue? It predominantly revolves around one's internal cognitive processes. The perceptions one holds greatly impact the functioning of the mind and possess a profoundly influential force.

Therefore, it is crucial to transcribe your desired life outcomes onto your vision board using present tense language, as though they have already been actualized. Subsequently, engage in a daily practice wherein you position yourself before the board and reverberate these affirmations akin to mantras, deliberately eliminating any extraneous thoughts. Progress from one sentence to another, effectively weaving the sentences together, thus cultivating a mindset that aligns with the persona you wish to embody.

Assuming that you have a desire to encounter your ideal partner. According to conventional wisdom, it can be inferred that you have not yet encountered your ideal life partner. That places you within the category of individuals who are in dire need, which is an inappropriate classification to be associated with. It is imperative to acknowledge that a gentleman of high standards will not be inclined towards women who display a sense of desperate pursuit. Temporarily shut your eyes and envisage yourself alongside him. Develop self-assurance in order to embrace your authentic self, aligning yourself with the partner who truly values and appreciates you, thus refraining from concealing your potential. The sorrow arising from being alone is not a prerequisite. If you genuinely desire to attract his attention, optimize your chances of becoming the individual that matches your ideal vision of Mr. Right, and incorporate this aspiration onto your prospective board.

- I possess all the qualities that are desired by an ideal partner.
- I possess a feminine and alluring demeanor, emanating an aura of self-assurance.
- I possess a strong sense of self-reliance and am highly deserving of affection.

Then, stop looking. To increase the likelihood of him being drawn towards you, maintain your faith in the belief that he will eventually locate you by continuing with your daily activities and affirming your true self. The ideal man you have in mind is not actively seeking a romantic connection with you. He is in search of the ideal female partner. Be that woman.

You have the ability to become whoever you desire. Regrettably, individuals possess a tendency to diminish their true capabilities and potential. The vision board facilitates the preservation of that belief, enabling you to embody your aspirations. This disparity is of significant magnitude as it emanates from the distinct mechanisms at play within your brain, thus illustrating its essentiality in determining one's achievement.

Four: Remind Yourself

It is beneficial to possess a tangible item or object that serves as a constant reminder of your vision on a daily basis. An instance featured in the film "Up" pertains to the character named Ellie. She created a compendium of her experiences in Paradise Falls, showcasing them through a meticulously crafted "Adventure Book" that showcases pasted photographs. Despite Ellie's demise, upon Carl's encounter with the adventure book, he was able to retrieve their shared vision.

There are methods available to assist in maintaining a constant awareness of one's aspirations.

Draw it. I am acquainted with an individual who aspires to establish an educational institution within a span of five years. She had presented to me an artistic rendering depicting her in the act of instructing within an educational institution. Although her drawing possessed a certain rawness, it did not reflect the depth and sophistication of her life's aspiration. She stows that illustration in her wallet and carries it with her wherever she traverses. The paper had already become significantly deteriorated. She has not yet obtained her school, however, I am confident that she is making progress towards achieving her objective.

Cut and paste pictures. Additionally, it is advantageous to possess visual representations that serve as reminders of your objective. If an image of your ideal home were to come to your attention, consider affixing it to your bedroom wall via cutting and taping. I am aware of an individual who expressed a desire to reduce their body weight. She observed an image of a woman possessing a flawless physique within the pages of a publication. She proceeded to dissect the corpse and affixed a photograph of her own visage onto it using adhesive tape. Therefore, whenever she experiences moments of discouragement, she simply gazes upon that image and envisions a future where her physique will come to resemble it.

Write it down. Compose your vision on paper and position it in a prominent location where it remains within your view on a daily basis. By doing so, you will be prompted to recollect your life's aspirations. Documenting your thoughts in a journal can also be immensely beneficial, particularly in the pursuit of objectives that span a substantial period of time. For instance, in the event that your objective is to acquire a residential property within the span of ten years, it becomes necessary to establish intermediary goals, such as annual or monthly milestones, to effectively progress toward the realization of your overarching ambition. Maintaining a journal will enable you to effectively monitor your progress towards achieving that objective, while simultaneously serving as a source of inspiration to persist in your endeavors. Disseminate it among an individual with similar interests and viewpoints. Communicating your aspirations and ambitions to an individual who shares the same perspective or genuinely cares about your wellbeing is an unequivocal method to sustain their vitality. That individual will serve as your collaborator in achieving the objective at hand and will assist you in its attainment. If your aspiration is to conquer Mount Everest, achieving this ambition would be greatly enhanced through the companionship of an individual who shares your profound passion for mountaineering.

Action Point:
Of the aforementioned proposed methods, which do you consider to be the most impactful for you?

_____

_____

Commence creating a memorandum outlining your vision and objectives in your life.

1

ARE VISUALS THAT IMPORTANT?

In a society such as ours, convenience forms the cornerstone of every aspect. Individuals tend to browse through a website solely if it is convenient. They solely partake in social gatherings, participate in formal assemblies, and adhere strictly to scheduled events that suit their requirements. Moreover, they possess the tendency to only retain information when it is conveniently presented. This is not solely our responsibility, indeed. This phenomenon can be attributed to the inherent tendency of the human brain to adopt shortcuts and exhibit a certain degree of laziness.

The human brain, in its inherent design, has a propensity to prioritize visuals over intricate textual information. Consequently, individuals are compelled to be drawn towards visuals and fully engrossed in a visual encounter. This phenomenon arises from the fact that among the majority of individuals possessing unimpaired visual systems, vision reigns supreme as the most influential sense. Our eyes possess an excess of one million nerve fibers, which effectively receive, decipher, and process the visual information with remarkable rapidity. Moreover, the human brain possesses a significant aptitude for retaining visual information more rapidly than written text and with minimal inaccuracies. Based on scientific evidence, it has been determined that the human brain possesses an inherent capability to process visual stimuli approximately 60,000 times faster compared to written text. This serves to demonstrate that while the comprehension of information conveyed in a 500-word text can be achieved within a few minutes, a visual representation has the capacity to accomplish the same comprehension in mere seconds, with a significant and enduring resonance.

The promising prospects of a visually appealing display

So, what are visuals? Are they that important? What is the etymology of these languages, and what led to their recognition as a means of communication? When we contemplate any type of artistic expression, these significant inquiries emerge in our thoughts. Given that Design is a discipline primarily concerned with visual communication, it is often the designers themselves who find themselves overwhelmed by this multitude of queries.

We consider a visual representation, whether it is a picture or an infographic, as a flat, two-dimensional plane typically adorned with various hues and forms. However, a picture embodies far more than that. An image can be regarded as a means of communication that surpasses language barriers. It effectively embodies the thoughts and principles of the creator, resulting in a heightened connection with the viewers and evoking a profound visual encounter.

Regarding design, there exists a meticulous and spirited utilization of color, lines, and shapes to effectively convey a message to the observer. It is expected that the recipients will acquire a specific notion upon observation of these graphical representations, and subsequently engage in a systematic examination of said information.

A significant majority, exceeding 91% of the global human population, displays a pronounced preference for visuals over textual content. This is the reason why data is universally presented in accessible, dynamic, and interactive visualizations, facilitating enhanced comprehension for the observer and considerably reducing time consumption. In our contemporary era characterized by a profusion of information, the significance of accessing information that is both efficient and precise cannot be overstated. Visuals serve as a highly effective means of communication. On each occasion that a designer presents a visual, they endeavor to transmit a message to the audience in a straightforward manner that is comprehensible to all. Whether it pertains to an artwork or an infographic, a designer will endeavor to effectively communicate the maximum amount of information possible. Designers frequently possess the ability to encapsulate abstract concepts that are arduous or imprecise to articulate through verbal means, and instead express them in a visual format. Visual aids aid us in promptly, efficiently, and convincingly disseminating profound and significant messages.

A visual representation has the potential to serve as a powerful catalyst, inciting individuals to adopt a specific mindset. Visual elements have a tendency to subliminally influence our cognitive processes, irrespective of our ability to consciously recall having perceived them. They possess significant influence and have the ability to entirely transform an individual's cognition. This is the reason why the discipline of Design acts as a convergence point for various facets of both artistic and scientific domains. The deliberate consideration of typography, color, shapes, layout, and size is paramount, as these elements significantly influence one's perception of an object or concept. By merely modifying the dimensions of textual elements or repositioning shapes, the interpretation of your visual representation can undergo significant transformations. With the mere utilization of a graphic or image, one possesses the capability to make a substantial influence on the world. That represents the level of influence exerted by a visual representation.

The utilization of imagery can elicit a specific impact on individuals. They have a proclivity to elicit distinct emotional responses in individuals, which are subject to variation depending on their idiosyncratic interpretations and personal histories. Hence, design holds distinct connotations for each individual. We have a tendency to regard aesthetically pleasing entities as attractive, as they elicit specific emotions within us. Individuals have an innate desire to possess objects of beauty that evoke a sense of uniqueness, thereby creating a perpetual ambiance of distinctive magnificence in their surroundings. The incorporation of visual elements within design has the potential to elicit a diverse range of emotions, encompassing serenity, excitement, and intrigue.

The emblem of the Olympic Games, consisting of five interlocking rings, serves as an exemplary illustration of a remarkably uncomplicated visual element that holds universal recognition. It elicits anticipation among spectators and fosters unwavering resolve in athletes who devote extensive periods of time to pursue the opportunity of achieving podium placement. Frequently, the individuals who emerge victorious will adorn their bodies with tattoos depicting the Olympic rings as a commemoration of the event.

THE IMPORTANCE OF DESIGN
A meticulously crafted visual possesses the capability to enhance our quality of life and simplify our decision-making

process, thus allowing us to allocate valuable time towards other significant undertakings. Design is pervasive in various aspects of our surroundings, encompassing road signs, smartwatches, and notably, graphical representations and tabular structures. Visual communication surpasses linguistic barriers and brings together individuals from across the globe through the power of images. One example to illustrate this point is that the arduous process of reading, interpreting, and scrutinizing a manual can be greatly simplified using a visual tool.

Reflect upon your most recent purchase of IKEA furniture. What was the duration of time it took for you to assemble? I trust that the duration of the matter was not unduly protracted, correct? Despite the shelf or desk taking longer than anticipated, consider the alternative of accomplishing it without any visual aids.

The use of imagery has exerted a considerable impact on human civilization from its inception. Prior to the development of human language, the human mind conceived visual modes of communication as a means to effectively convey ideas to others. Throughout human history, ranging from the era of our earliest ancestors to the modern age, different forms of visual representation have been employed, each imbued with its own distinct significance, purpose, and rationale. Throughout history, ample evidence exists to illustrate how visual stimuli possess the capacity to engender transformation and elicit a myriad of emotions within an individual. As an illustration, within the context of the Romantic era, artists who were profoundly impacted by conflicts and widespread violence turned to visual mediums as a means to convey their anguish, sorrow, and suffering. These visual depictions not only conveyed the artist's thoughts and emotions but also facilitated viewers' ability to empathize with and subsequently express their own similar sentiments.

Another great example is Picasso\'s famous painting \"Guernica\" which he painted after the Spanish Civil War in 1937. This exceptional work of art meticulously and earnestly conveyed the profound horrors, psychological wounds, and indirect repercussions inflicted upon the inhabitants of Guernica in the aftermath of warfare. The massive monochromatic artwork proficiently illustrates the depletion of vibrant colors from a post-war world. The artwork emphasizes the depiction of satiated creatures, women expressing distress, an eyeball, flames, and a mutilated soldier. These various elements not solely depict the impact of war on multiple entities ranging from humans to animals, but also acknowledge and give voice to the anguish experienced by each individual. This serves as a compelling illustration demonstrating the ability of a powerful and significant visual representation to effectively engage individuals on an emotional plane.

Avid supporter
Regardless of whether a visual is employed to facilitate the sale of a commercial product, advocate for a non-profit organization, or convey statistics of a news program, an effective design possesses the ability to harmonize individuals towards a shared objective.
In addition, the field of design exerts a direct influence on individuals' lives as it

shapes the very fabric of our built environment through constant innovation. In a society of such nature, it is rendered unfeasible to sustain an autonomous existence bereft of intentional design. A formidable force that holds the capacity to influence choices and evoke deep-seated emotions within an individual should not be disregarded. It is imperative to leverage it to your benefit.

Six: Elucidation of Creative Visualization as Expounded by Wallace Wattles

In his acclaimed literary work "The Science of Getting Rich (1910)," Wallace Wattles expounds upon the notion of visualization. Every person with a vested interest in the power of the human mind is acquainted with him or has perused this literary work. "The Science of Getting Rich (1910)" has achieved remarkable acclaim and remains one of the most extensively examined literary works to this day. This book continues to enjoy the same level of popularity it possessed a century ago.

In his seminal work, 'The Science of Getting Rich (1910)', the author expounds upon his contemplations and revelations regarding the acquisition of wealth, or the attainment of any desired object or outcome. Wattles formulated the concept of inventive visualization and effectively spearheaded a movement centered around this cognitive practice. He served as a source of inspiration for numerous authors, among them Napoleon Hill. The primary basis of the book and the movie "The Secret" revolved around the author's profound understandings of the concept of creative visualization.

As per the teachings of Wallace Wattles, it is posited that all facets of our existence originate from our thoughts. The functioning of the cosmos is intrinsically linked to the power of human cognition, whereby our thoughts possess the potential to manifest and materialize into tangible realities.

According to Wallace's book, if we perceive ourselves residing in a recently constructed abode, donning elegant garments, and utilizing an automobile for our everyday commutes, we can harbor unwavering assurance in all aspects of our lives. He recommends envisioning an ideal environment or achieving monetary stability in a manner that aligns with your desires, and subsequently experiencing each of these envisioned scenarios repeatedly. According to his perspective, this will effectively facilitate the desired transformation in our lives.

Wattles commented that by aligning one's thoughts with an established thought process or belief, one has the ability to exert influence over the manifestation or generation of the substance upon which they concentrate.

As per his perspective, it is essential to maintain unwavering concentration on one's objectives until they are ultimately realized. The individual should persistently contemplate this matter and come to terms with it as an unyielding truth. Once you have made a decision regarding your goal, commence cultivating the mindset that it is already within your possession or in the process of being achieved. Give it thorough consideration and reflection for the purpose of aligning your thoughts with the universe, thereby solidifying it as your perceived reality.

Ensure clarity regarding your objective and consistently contemplate it in your thoughts. Refrain from contemplating upon current situations or circumstances, as they may impede your progress towards achieving success.

According to the teachings of Wallace Wattles, it is essential for individuals to express gratitude for their current possessions and circumstances. Expressing gratitude forges a connection with the inherent force within oneself. Individuals may ascribe the appellation of God, the Spirit, or the Divine to it. This energy or connection is in fact the catalyst for the transformation or realization of visualization. Expressions of appreciation unlock the energetic centers of your being and expose you to a state of receptiveness or willingness to consider various perspectives.

Wallace Wattles asserts that various factors converge to determine one's success in life. Therefore, it is imperative that you express gratitude for all the elements that have indeed played a significant role in fostering your accomplishments.

The Profound Expression Of Appreciation

The third phase of the creative visualization procedure involves recognition and appreciation. In order for visualization to be effective, it is necessary to take stock of one's blessings. It is essential to recognize and value the present circumstances and any incremental achievements encountered along the path towards one's desired existence.

When one experiences gratitude, a sense of well-being ensues, consequently expediting the manifestation of one's goals and dreams by the universe.

Regularly contemplate the things for which you express gratitude. Express gratitude for the presence of nourishment upon your dining surface, for the possession of gainful employment, and for the provision of shelter above your dwelling. Express gratitude for those individuals in your vicinity, namely your life partner, parents, siblings, acquaintances, and colleagues. Appreciate opportunities. Embrace and acknowledge the value of all the possessions within your possession at present - your dwelling, vehicle, electronic devices, mobile phone, attire, furnishings, domestic equipment, and valuable adornments. Appreciate your body. Ensure that you handle it with utmost care.

The majority of individuals experience dissatisfaction due to their tendency to overlook the value of things they have. They fail to acknowledge the value of their current possessions. They consistently assess the glass with a pessimistic perspective, perceiving it as being half-empty. Thankful individuals consistently view their glass as half full.

The effectiveness of visualization is compromised when one experiences a sense of insufficiency. One must possess a sense of gratitude in order to recognize and appreciate the blessings bestowed upon them.

Outlining
Outlining entails specifying to a higher power the precise manner in which one desires an outcome to materialize. This practice is commonly referred to as outlining. Excessive specificity can

inadvertently hinder the attainment of desirable outcomes.

One additional significant rationale for abstaining from outlining is the possibility that your aspirations may not align with the grand design orchestrated by the Universe.

A new vehicle was requested by one of my clientele. She approached me with her aspiration and subsequently elucidated the manner in which it would manifest in her life.

Her strategy commenced by making a visit to a car dealership, engaging in a test drive of the automobile, and subsequently receiving an offer of payment that aligned with her financial means, albeit barely so. I attentively listened to her and, rather than providing a detailed description of how a new car would materialize, I advised her to begin with envisioning the desired vehicle as the solution. She ceased delineating the object and redirected her attention solely towards the automobile. After the passage of three weeks, her aunt initiated communication with her. Due to her aunt's inability to drive, she expressed a desire to bestow upon her the very car she had envisioned.

Abstain from outlining; instead, employ visualization techniques to envision your desired outcome. Start with the answer. Place your trust in the Universe to provide what you long for.

An additional instance of delineation is the crafting of a treasure map by an individual with the intention of securing an affectionate companion. These maps contain aesthetically pleasing illustrations depicting the methods and locations for encountering one's ideal life partner, leading to a magical love story culminating in a joyous matrimony. Engaging in the creation of treasure maps can be an enjoyable endeavor; however, it is advisable to exercise caution in regards to excessive specificity. For example, one might idealize a magical encounter during a holiday trip and inadvertently overlook the gentleman who regularly takes the elevator in the office building they work at.

Engaging in cartographic exploration can provide enjoyment, however, it is crucial to maintain receptiveness towards numerous potential outcomes. I would kindly suggest that you commence with providing the answer, allowing the Universe to undertake the strenuous work involved.

I consistently advise incorporating the phrase, "May this or a more desirable outcome manifest in my reality," into every prayer or affirmation. By doing so, you open yourself up to the possibilities that surpass your present imagination, enabling the Universe to deliver an outcome surpassing your expectations.

Utter your affirmation with unwavering faith, resolute determination, and unwavering concentration on the intended fruition of your aspiration. Instead of explicitly stating your desires, remain receptive to the possibilities that the Universe may unveil to you.

If you apply potent positive energy to your affirmations and subsequently transmit them to the Universe with serenity and assurance, I can guarantee that the Universe will reciprocate.

Hate

Hostility is a substantial obstacle that will prevent positive outcomes from entering your life, exerting a detrimental influence on both your well-being and financial situation. The presence of hatred infiltrates every aspect of your life and extends its negative influence onto the lives of those around you.

Adverse emotions pertaining to oneself or others possess the capability to impede the realization of one's aspirations. Disdain engenders a substantial obstruction of significant magnitude.

Feelings of hatred, refusal to forgive, or harboring negative thoughts and emotions towards oneself or others serve as impediments to any positive outcomes and restrict the abundance that could otherwise manifest in one's life.

Expressing animosity or harboring discriminatory attitudes towards any particular group, ethnicity, faith, or sexual orientation will impede your personal growth and well-being.

On one occasion while engaged in a professional client interaction, we conducted a thorough analysis of her cognitive processes and evaluative attitudes towards individuals in her social sphere. She perceived herself to be fortunate in most aspects of her life, save for the presence of a neighbor who harbored contrasting political ideologies. She displayed a vehement animosity towards the political signs on her neighbor's property and harbored a strong dislike for the candidate. During our conversation, she came to the realization that harboring animosity towards her neighbor was acting as a hindrance to the attainment of her desired well-being. Ultimately, she arrived at the conclusion that harboring dislike towards her neighbor or the candidate proved to be unworthy of her efforts.

Upon venting her frustration, she experienced a sense of tranquility. Tranquility enveloped her abode, and the desired blessings commenced to manifest. By remarkable chance, the signs in her yard were voluntarily removed by her neighbor, without any instigation.

Hatred obstructs the natural flow of exchanges and extends its negative influence across all aspects of your existence. Formally phrased: "Harboring enmity towards an individual, whether in the past or present, leads to a disruption of equilibrium." Hatred impedes the unrestricted circulation of affection and positivity within your life. Antipathy impedes the functioning of the Law of Attraction.

Let go of any detrimental emotions that hinder your ability to embrace positivity. Reside within an environment devoid of critical assessment.

At any given moment, one can experience only a single emotion. The aforementioned emotions can be categorized as either affection or apprehension. Fear presents itself in the form of hatred, resentment, and various unfavorable emotions.

Abandon fear, relinquish anger, release regret, and establish love as the cornerstone of cultivating a more robust, more content, and more prosperous life.

Cord Cutting

Occasionally, there appears to be an intangible factor impeding our progress towards achieving success.

Although we may lack awareness regarding the underlying reason, we are aware of the resultant outcome. The causation eludes us.

If that is indeed the case, it is possible that we are interconnected by an enduring Etherical Cord, connecting us to a distant memory within our present existence or conceivably from a previous lifetime.

I perceive ethereal cords as delicate, refined, shimmering, silver-hued conduits that exude an enchanting radiance, spanning the distance between ourselves and the individuals we hold dear. Although many are unable to perceive these intangible cords, we can perceive their presence as they establish an emotional connection between ourselves and those who hold affection towards us and vice versa. We can perceive their presence when we perceive that a beloved individual is undergoing distress or perhaps facing perils.

Furthermore, these cords serve to connect us to various experiences, locations, and possessions.

Intangible bonds link us to both cherished acquaintances and unknown individuals with whom we experience an immediate affinity. We have swiftly developed a strong sense of acquaintance with these individuals; it appears as though we have been acquainted with them for the entirety of our existence. No instances of unease arise when interacting with these newfound companions, and even periods of silence feel effortlessly comfortable.

The French expression déjà vu, which translates to "already seen," refers to the phenomenon where one feels as though they have experienced something before. Etherical Cords are instances of déjà vu that are also perceptible.

Etherical Cords have the potential to tether us to distressing encounters, damaging associations, and distressful incidents. Similar to individuals who have experienced the trauma of war and are affected by post-traumatic stress disorder, the onset of an intrusive sound has the ability to transport us back to the distressing memories associated with the event. Occasionally, those recollections may originate from our present existence or extend across several centuries.

Have you ever encountered individuals who possess an innate fear of water, fire, or heights, devoid of any personal encounters or prior knowledge in this present existence to substantiate such apprehension? These apprehensions and alarming recollections may not have originated from a childhood incident, but rather, from a past existence experienced several centuries in the past.

Occasionally, the disquieting visions that manifest in one's dreams are not categorized as mere nightmares or the result of an overly vivid imagination; rather, they bear the weight of being recollections.

Whether it be in the present or in a past existence, it is possible for us to retain suppressed memories or experiences of such profundity that they elude our conscious recollection. However, the ethereal connection and its impact will persist until we let go of these distressing occurrences.

During a past professional collaboration, I discerned that a previous romantic involvement was impeding the personal growth and ability to fully embrace the affectionate connections sought after by a captivating young lady. I discerned her enduring attachment to the potent ethereal connection she had forged between her tormenting suitor and the recollections she retained of him.

"Inquiring whether he occupies your thoughts on a frequency of more than three instances weekly," I inquired.

She laughed. I find myself pondering his presence every hour, thrice.

She was bound to a relationship that had concluded years ago. The distressing nature of the relationship was hindering her ability to partake in the affectionate relationship she currently desired.

Through the identification of this detrimental connection, we commenced efforts to sever this detrimental bond. Multiple instances of cord cutting were necessary to completely sever this particular connection. During the course of our collaboration, she also acquired the ability to recalibrate her energy in order to attract a compassionate partner who would shower her with affection and demonstrate profound regard. After a span of several weeks, she ultimately achieved success. Coincidentally, a gentleman who embodied all of her aspirations materialized in her life. Presently, she is residing in a state of perpetual happiness alongside a newlywed spouse, who deeply cherishes and wholeheartedly encourages her aspirations.

Some ethereal cords may lack easy identifiability. As an illustration, we could have pledged vows of destitution in a previous existence, when we embodied roles of monasticism, clergy, or within a sacred fraternity. I took a solemn oath of embracing a life of austerity in the eleventh century, and have carried this commitment with me into the present incarnation. I found it necessary to eliminate those commitments in order to establish a renewed sense of financial prosperity in my life.

If any of these words or experiences strike a chord with you, it may be necessary to sever a connection. There is no necessity for you to recollect the precise moment when you made such a solemn promise or revisit a previous existence. It is sufficient to have an awareness of its presence.

Performing the act of severing a cord need not entail a convoluted ritual. Indeed, the concept can be easily understood.

In my professional practice, I engage in a spiritual connection with Archangels. Therefore, when the need arises to detach myself from individuals, locations, or objects that are not beneficial to my well-being, I respectfully appeal to Archangel Michael. I beseech him to employ his symbolic fiery sword as a means to sever any energetic connections that may hinder my growth and progress. Following the severance of energetic attachments, I consistently call upon Archangel Raphael to apply his restorative green healing light in order to facilitate the full recovery process.

For certain ethereal connections, a single act of severing the cord will suffice. Additional cables are robust and possess the ability to regenerate. Should this scenario arise, it is imperative to acknowledge that certain circumstances may require multiple interventions before they are entirely resolved. Sever ties until you are liberated from individuals or distressing recollections that continue to torment you. They do not possess any relevance within the context of your present existence.

There exists a multitude of diverse approaches to cord-cutting. Please locate an option that aligns with your personal preferences and instinctual judgement.

If you find it necessary to reach out to a professional, there are a number of excellent metaphysical practitioners available who can provide assistance with internet-based cord cutting.

Preserve the affectionate, splendid bonds that connect you to sincere relationships, while severing any bonds that restrain you or hinder your ability to embrace prosperity.

On a daily basis, I implore you to engage in the practice of meditation, establishing a profound connection with the Universe to heighten your state of consciousness. Examine the notions and convictions that impede your progress towards achieving success. On a daily basis, I implore you to allocate a period of time for contemplation and mental imagery.

You possess the inherent capacity to achieve greatness; your very nature is predisposed to manifest extraordinary outcomes. It's your birthright.

In the subsequent , I will elucidate on the method to expedite the attainment of your aspirations through the fervent influence of Heaven.

Could You Provide Detailed Guidance On The Process Of Visualization And Its Integration Into One's Schedule?

You can harness the benefits of visualization in your everyday life by utilizing the following techniques:

Determine the Influence of Memories on Your Being

If you happen to have memories that are causing distress, endeavor to ascertain their impacts on your life. It is possible that you may encounter challenges in experiencing restful slumber, or these occurrences may evoke feelings of dread on a consistent basis. In the initial stage, it would be advantageous to ascertain the effects of these variables on your well-being. Consider the discernible transformations that manifest in your life subsequent to traumatic occurrences. If you are experiencing symptoms of tension, anxiety, respiratory difficulties, or insomnia, it would be advisable to actively participate in physical exercises as a means of alleviating such conditions. The practice of meditation and mindfulness may prove to be a suitable option for you. Engage in a morning stroll to inhale the invigorating air and contemplate the unparalleled splendor of nature.

Direct your attention towards the future. Constantly dwelling on past events and distressing memories can have detrimental effects on one's mental well-being. It is not possible to retroactively correct these matters. It would be beneficial to engage in strenuous physical activities as a means of diverting your attention. You have the opportunity to arrange social engagements with companions on a weekly basis, while contemplating your professional aspirations and personal ambitions. Ensure that you actively involve yourself in future endeavors, as this will gradually alleviate the distress associated with your past experiences.

Learn New Habits

Writing can serve as a beneficial and constructive means to alleviate oneself from the weight of recollections that bear emotional distress from past experiences. You may choose to expound upon past recollections, delving into their profound influences on your personal existence. It can assist in accessing pertinent emotions and retrieving accurate memories. Make an effort to acquire fresh habits to ensure the continual engagement of both your body and mind. These novel practices have the potential to enhance your existence, enabling you to effectively navigate the obstacles that come your way.

Joyful habits

In order to overcome distressing recollections, it is advisable to cultivate more constructive experiences as they prove more advantageous to your well-being. Cultivate novel behaviors to acquire fresh memories, as the distressing recollections have the potential to be detrimental to one's well-being. Make an effort to cultivate a circle of individuals who exude happiness and have the ability to infuse your life with joy. Ensure you actively seek out an appropriate collective or pursuit to maintain cognitive and physical stimulation.

Change Your Routines

Consistently following a prescribed schedule can prompt introspection regarding the past, impeding one's ability to progress. It is imperative to enhance the enjoyment in one's life through the alteration of one's routine. Make an effort to engage in activities and incorporate novel experiences and individuals into your daily routine. Make an effort to connect with individuals capable of bolstering your newfound habits. It would be beneficial to venture into novel activities, such as enrolling in a yoga or martial arts course. Endeavor to maintain a distance from circumstances that may potentially evoke recollections of your past. One may seek the assistance of a dependable sibling, spouse, parent, or a trusted individual to engage in a dialogue and seek input in order to alleviate the presence of recollections.

GUIDED GRATITUDE MEDITATION

For the narrator's convenience, it is kindly requested to allocate a time gap of 15 seconds between each sentence, unless specified otherwise. The vocal demeanor should be calming, yet not excessively unhurried.

Prior to commencing, locate a suitable environment where interruptions are unlikely, and ensure that all electronic devices are powered off.

Assume a comfortable seated or reclined position. If it is possible, kindly shut your eyes or direct your attention towards an object situated in your immediate vicinity.

Allow your entire body to achieve a state of relaxation by fully releasing tension, grounding your weight into the floor, elongating both your legs and spine, and intentionally easing the tension in every muscle.

Take deliberate, gentle breaths and endeavor to clear your mind by attentively acknowledging and releasing each thought as it arises. Recite this procedure whenever you sense a drifting of your focus during the course of the meditation.

Now, proceed to take in a breath through your oral cavity at your customary rate. Subsequently, retain the breath for a duration of four counts, following which, gradually release it through your oral cavity.

Continue to execute this sequence, whereby you inhale deeply, retain your breath for a count of four (one, two, three, four), and gradually exhale the air from your lungs.

Breathe in deeply, then maintain the breath for a count of four before exhaling (Repeat this process at 15-second intervals for a total duration of two minutes).

Release any tension or stress accumulated throughout the day.

Expand your capacity for empathy and open your cognitive faculties by envisioning a radiant illumination permeating through the crown of your head and surging throughout your entire being.

Now, I kindly request that you revisit your recollections of yesterday's meditative state, when you were positioned within the specified room, directly facing the reflective surface.

If you so desire, you have the option to utilize the word you have chosen previously, which will expedite your journey to the desired location.

Make an effort to recapture those positive emotions, the boundless positive vitality that coursed through you as you commemorated your essence and true identity.

Allow the identical energy to flow through your being at present, refraining from attempting to impede or regulate it. Embrace total self-surrender, allowing the energy to envelop you with a sense of being desired and cherished.

Allow the illumination to permeate your being, experiencing the profound affection and appreciation for your current state and future potential. Cherish yourself.

Immerse yourself in an abundance of positive emotions and allow them to flow through every fiber of your being, encircling you with their radiant aura of affection and positivity.

Allow them to make contact with each individual area of your physique, commencing with the extremities of your feet.

Please take a moment to express your appreciation to every component, as they consistently devote their efforts to serving and meeting your every requirement, diligently and unceasingly, throughout each passing moment of each day.

Commence by focusing on your feet, gradually extending and relaxing them, expressing gratitude for their unwavering support.

Now proceed to the area encompassing your lower extremities. Engage in muscle stretching exercises to experience a surging vitality that empowers you to embark on your daily endeavors unhindered. Breathe out, and direct affection and appreciation towards them.

Ascend to the level of your midsection, attentively experiencing the functioning of each internal organ to promote your physical and mental wellness.

Take a deliberate and gentle breath inward, and, as you release your breath, direct affectionate and compassionate energy towards each individual involved.

Proceed to elongate your spinal column and experience the support it offers to your entire physique. Extend your heartfelt affection and appreciation towards it as you inhale and exhale at a gentle pace.

Engage in arm and hand movements such as shaking and stretching. Express gratitude to individuals for their acceptance and engagement in the experience of living, and subsequently extend appreciation towards the intellect and consciousness. Kindly read at a slower pace, allowing for a brief pause between each segment.

Now, take a few moments to reflect upon and recollect the multitude of challenges that your body successfully surmounted in order to culminate in this present moment.

Convey your affection and appreciation for everything that has transpired and for all the future occurrences that lie ahead.

Experience the profound envelopment of affection coursing within your being at this moment, and observe how this sentiment fundamentally enhances its well-being, fortifying it for any upcoming endeavors.

Allow it to overflow from within you and permeate every crevice of this enclosure, where you reside with security and protection.

Gently visualize interacting with every item in the room, bestowing upon each a heartfelt blessing, thereby honoring every memory and meaningful bond attached to them. (Allow for a brief pause of 30 seconds.) "

Inhale the collective affection present within the space, allowing it to permeate your being and resonate within your heart.

Observe how boundless affection emanates from this space, permeating the streets and illuminating them with its radiant essence.

Witness its permeation throughout each and every corner, edifice within your urban center, and extending into the realm beyond.

Allow the inherent positivity within you to emanate from your being, permeating the world and disseminating your radiant influence far and wide.

May it have an impact on each individual who has provided encouragement, support, and affection to you over the course of time.

Visualize the countenance of each individual, even those hailing from a remote historical epoch, and express benevolence and appreciation towards them, as you simultaneously receive their reciprocated sentiments.

Kindly ensure no hesitation in expressing your love and gratitude, as they shall be reciprocated manifold.

Allow them to soar unrestricted until they have traversed every corner of this globe.

Observe how your affection bestows blessings and nurtures the depths of your heart, revitalizing tranquility and enhancing the grace that was once diminished.

Express gratitude for all that is positive on this Earth, encompassing the myriad offerings presented to you on a daily basis, and the awe-inspiring splendor that encompasses your surroundings.

Transmit aspirations and affection towards your future self, with the intent of constructing pathways for novel experiences and forthcoming opportunities.

Mentally envision even the minutest details for which gratitude is warranted, and transmit expressions of gratefulness to them.

Reconnect with all that is benevolent and affectionate in this world, relinquishing all attachments that currently confine and prevent you from savoring the present moment.

Allow yourself to soar propelled by the immense power of love; envelop yourself in its embrace.

Show appreciation for your current self and for the potential of your future self.

Experience the reciprocation of your affection and appreciation, as the moments cherished and the bond strengthened.

Allow yourself to embrace these feelings and find pleasure in this sensation.

Should you desire, you may also choose to mentally recite your confidential word thrice, in order to enhance the preservation of this moment within you. (A brief intermission.)

Now, redirect your attention towards your breathing.

Please position your hands on your lower abdomen, and, during inhalation, experience the subtle inward movement of your belly towards your spine.

While expelling the breath, perceive its gradual restoration to its initial state.

Once more, take a deep breath, allowing your abdomen to contract as you inhale, and then exhale slowly as you allow your abdomen to expand.

As you engage in respiration, perceive the flow of energy coursing throughout your physique, directing your concentration towards any impediment or region of distress that persists within you.

Please take note of these locations as we will be addressing them in the subsequent leg of our journey.

Continue to engage in controlled breathing by maintaining a slow and deliberate rhythm, ensuring you breathe in and out while placing your hand on your abdominal region.

Savor the tranquility and serenity, the motionlessness of your physical being.

Once more perceive the pulsation of your heart and the coursing of blood within your veins.

Deliberately elongate and rhythmically rouse each region of your physique, commencing from the base and progressively ascending to the apex.

Return to the room and commence experiencing the tactile sensation of the ground beneath your feet, as well as the auditory stimuli surrounding you.

Please allocate a brief duration of time to return your full attention to the current moment. I would like to take a momentary break of 30 seconds.

Once you are prepared, proceed to uncover your eyes or shift your focus away from the object you were previously fixated upon and direct it to your current surroundings.

Please rise and gently tap your feet on the floor to reestablish grounding.

Sensitize yourself to the encompassing affection and appreciation; reciprocate by bestowing your own love and gratitude upon the Universe.

We express gratitude for your attentiveness during today's meditation session.

The Power Of Visualization

Visualization entails directing one's focus and mental energy towards a prevailing thought. A notion possesses magnetic energy that draws in other energies of a similar nature. Every occurrence in our existence, as well as all our possessions, originated from a basic cognitive process. We can observe the manifestation of this principle in instances where an individual entertains persistent thoughts about a friend, and consequently, serendipitously encounters them or receives a corresponding communication via phone or email. The efficacy of visualization will have been in operation. By engaging in deliberate thinking and consistently maintaining that thinking in our consciousness, we manifest and materialize that thought through the process of mental imagery. If one maintains a constant belief that they are unwell, they are more likely to manifest illness. If one believes that they possess contentment, they will undoubtedly draw joy towards themselves. Hence, deliberate mental imagery concerning our desired outcomes in life can facilitate their manifestation in our existence. This exemplifies the efficacy of visualization.

Visualization: Crafting a Mental Map for Achieving Success

To commence the construction of a edifice, an architect must initially conceptualize the desired form and structure. The aforementioned mental representation is subsequently depicted onto a physical medium: a blueprint. The constructors implement whichever concepts have been engraved on the architectural plan. Visual representation functions in an identical manner. The cognitive representation that you possess of yourself within the depths of your subconsciousness materializes as an actuality in your existence.

STRATEGIES TO ENHANCE THE EFFICACY OF VISUALIZATION

Utilizing visualization can be efficacious at any given moment, including during one's daily routine; however, its maximum potency is realized when practiced in a state of relaxation. This is because the state of relaxation facilitates the access of your mental images to your subconscious mind. Initially, one attains a state of ease with closed eyes, followed by the release of any pessimistic convictions or emotions pertaining to the subject at hand. Subsequently, one should proceed by incorporating favorable visual representations and positive statements in order to recondition the mind with constructive and optimistic beliefs and visions of achieving success.

EVERYONE VISUALIZES DIFFERENTLY

The thought processes of individuals vary, so there is no need for concern if you do not experience a vivid mental picture or image. Occasionally, visualizations can be quite nuanced. If you possess a propensity for conceptual thinking, you may not perceive intricacies in visual presentation. Alternatively, you may be presented with impressions, concepts, emotions, or intuitive insights, or you may apprehend information through auditory perception within your subconscious mind. If you possess a propensity for visual cognition, you may opt to occlude your visual perception and conjure forth vibrant mental 'cinematographic' displays - comprising intricate depictions, hues, and visualizations. Alternatively, you may be presented with a blend of both visual representations and perceptions. It is advisable to refrain from forming anticipations regarding the appearance of your visualizations. Rigid expectations or concerns regarding the correctness of your actions often hinder the formation of impressions. Relax. Maintain a state of complete openness and receptivity to whatever arises within your inner thoughts. Your personal experiences will be singularly marvelous.

Throughout your sessions of visualization, it is possible to encounter various thoughts and images that appear unrelated to your desired self-image. Nevertheless, these notions and visuals may possess connections with other facets of your existence that bear relevance to the perception you hold of yourself. As they emerge, they may evoke particular emotions, and you might desire to document such imagery throughout your journey as a means of conveying the sentiments. When initially visualizing a new behavior or characteristic, one may encounter internal resistance, manifesting as contradictory thoughts such as "I could never possess such confidence" or "This is not compatible with my true nature". This phenomenon arises from the ingrained subconscious programming that has been prevalent for an extended duration. As you persist in engaging in the practice of visualization, this phenomenon will diminish and be supplanted by the constructive concepts that you are presently imbuing into your consciousness. As you engage in your daily sessions consistently, the progressive transformations in your life will become increasingly substantial.

REPETITION

The subconscious mind is impressed by the act of repetition. The continual inundation of your subconscious mind with optimistic concepts will ultimately lead to the erosion of power and dissolution of any negative notions. If feasible, endeavor to engage in at least one visualization per day. By diligently applying this technique, you will be astounded by the enhanced development of your capacity to visualize in your distinctive manner.

The Role of the Subconscious Mind in Visualization

One has the capability to employ their conscious mind and thoughts in order to steer and exert control over their subconscious mind. Your subconscious mind is in control of proceedings. Regardless of your awareness, your conscious mind is actively perceiving the thoughts that are being generated by your subconscious mind. To manifest your conscious desires, it is essential to actively engage your conscious mind in shaping the fundamental beliefs and conditioning of your subconscious mind. This can be readily accomplished through the application of imaginative visualization and the principle of the Law of Attraction. It is imperative that you direct your attention towards your well-defined vision of your authentic desires. This method is among the most straightforward and expeditious approaches to altering restrictive beliefs residing within the subconscious. The most efficacious approach to altering those constraining beliefs is to exemplify the change that you desire to observe in the world.

It ultimately boils down to one's true identity. Existence revolves around embodying the qualities of this individual. It is essential to recognize that, as individuals imbued with human capacity, we are responsible for the creation of machines. However, the manner in which this creation is executed begs consideration. We turn inward to our mental faculties, a formidable aspect of our being that materializes our thoughts into tangible existence. We have the ability to manifest our thoughts in the invisible realm.

You possess two components within your mind: one being the conscious element, while the other comprises the subconscious element. The subconscious component can be likened to a computer hard drive, as it is responsible for the execution of various functions, acting as a program. Hence, there exists a program lodged within your subconscious mind that governs all decision-making processes, and it is possible that this program does not consist of elements that are beneficial to you. Alternatively, it could be speculated that the predetermined path could prove inadequate in achieving one's desired destination, owing to the profound influence of an individual's ingrained beliefs and experiences over the course of their lifetime. Consequently, you may experience deliberate cognitions such as, "I aspire to enhance my financial status," "I strive to attain improved wellness," or similar aspirations. One may not merely entertain those notions, but rather approach them with utmost sincerity and engage in the practice of affirmations. However, if one does not engage in the training of the subconscious mind, the conscious mind, which is responsible for carrying out actions, becomes ineffective. It is imperative to attune the subconscious mind to a state of alignment with one's desired path, achieved through the act of envisioning one's desired physical manifestation. Continuously advance that vision, subsequently transitioning into the actuality of that vision.

When such an occurrence takes place, it signifies the embodiment of a life of nobility. It can be effortlessly accomplished if comprehended within this framework, yet it is an ongoing endeavor. Due to the incessant influx of stimuli emanating from various sources, such inundation is inherent to and constitutes the essence of this game. You have the privilege of selecting and sorting what is advantageous and what is not advantageous for you.

Subconscious Mind's Characteristics

The subconscious mind exhibits approximately seven distinct attributes:

1. The primary duty of the entity is to gather and assimilate all available information within its cognitive or sensory capabilities. Regardless of the quality, correctness, or validity of the information or input it receives, it is insignificant. Its sole purpose is to assimilate all information in an all-encompassing manner, akin to the absorption capacity of a sponge.

2. This particular characteristic of the subconscious is arguably one of its most significant attributes, akin to that of a four-year-old child. The psychological state of our subconscious mind bears resemblance to that of a juvenile individual. It endeavors to offer assistance to you to the best of its ability, akin to the way a child strives to do so. However, it lacks the knowledge or means to do so, even though it possesses the capability to bring about any

conceivable alteration. It is imperative that it receives appropriate instructions.

3. It will bestow upon you that which you are primarily experiencing and directing your attention towards. Envision this scenario as akin to an uncontrollable genie. On average, an individual typically has around 64,000 thoughts in a day. There are numerous thoughts that one becomes conscious of contemplating. Certain events occur spontaneously, while others originate from unwelcome thoughts or repulsive ideas. Furthermore, there are instances when one's thoughts revolve around dislikable subjects or matters that evoke strong aversion. Conversely, there are also instances when thoughts are centered on cherished emotions or objects of affection. Throughout the course of the day, a myriad of divergent thoughts occupy your mind. Whichever

objects capture your attention, the subconscious psyche shall deliver to you similar to a mystical entity. It constantly provides you with all that you are concentrating on. It is crucial to comprehend the significance of this matter; when contemplating upon the subject of your focus. You\\\'re focusing on money. When considering the reasons behind your inability to settle your financial obligations, what aspects are you giving your attention to? You are unable to meet your financial obligations. Consequently, the issue of insufficient funds to remunerate them will arise.

4. There exists an additional significant notion that the subconscious mind lacks awareness of past or future; it solely resides in the present. This will assist you in comprehending the origins of numerous issues. According to the

subconscious mind past, present, and future are all the same. It doesn\\\'t understand them. Hence, the present moment encompasses all opportunities. When you express the desire for money, your attention is ultimately directed towards its absence. When your attention is directed towards the objective of attaining health, where exactly is your focal point? Your attention is primarily directed towards a state of inadequate well-being. Now, as we embark on this endeavor, many individuals frequently express their desires and subsequently find themselves perplexed by the unintended outcomes they receive. The reason behind this lies in their fixation on the absence of it. And naturally, given the subconscious mind possesses an uncontrollable nature akin to a capricious genie, that is precisely the outcome you will obtain. It appears that you consistently satisfy your desires, obtaining the objects or outcomes you have sought. This can be achieved through deliberate intention, intentional consideration of the opposite, or prospective contemplation. It is difficult to ascertain the specific focus on which you may have been directing your attention. However, if your focus had not been directed towards attaining it in the present moment, it is likely that you have been inadvertently acting in contradiction to your desired outcome.

5. The subconscious mind lacks comprehension of the negative. Consider this perspective: a small exercise is currently underway. Please refrain from entertaining the notion of a lavishly attired primate of a violet hue engaging in a jubilant display of acrobatics atop your workstation, whilst aptly strumming a banjo. Don\\\'t think of it.

Have you given it any thought? Undoubtedly, you did, as there is truly no conceivable way to omit such consideration. To avoid contemplation of a certain matter, one must direct their thoughts toward the specific aspects that should be avoided. When you inform a child about the presence of a delicate crystal glass filled with water, their immediate thought is predominantly influenced by the instruction not to drop it, thus accentuating the negative aspect. Please refrain from continuing that action. It does not comprehend the negative implications. What is your initial reaction when you find yourself walking through a room and encounter someone in the process of changing in a corner who then instructs you not to look? Is it not to observe or ascertain their actions? The subconscious mind does not comprehend negativity. Therefore, when one's attention is primarily directed towards avoiding financial instability, physical ailment, inadequate payment of debts, and any other concerns. When engaging in these counterproductive behaviors, it fails to comprehend. Your attention appears to be directed towards drawing in the antithesis of your desired outcome. Therefore, your subconscious mind assumes the role of an obstinate controller. This outcome can generate an inability to meet financial obligations, deteriorate health conditions, and engross your attention in adverse circumstances. Hence, the system exclusively comprehends affirmative responses and inadvertently elicits adverse or contradictory outcomes when the word NO is employed.

6. The subconscious mind lacks the ability to comprehend sarcasm. What is sarcasm? It constitutes a light-hearted

manner of disparaging an individual. Indeed, there is hardly any necessity for it, as one must ponder the level of comprehension a child of merely four years would possess towards sarcasm. They just wouldn\\\'t understand.

7. The subconscious mind lacks the capacity to comprehend humor. When was the most recent occasion on which you communicated a joke in a comprehensible manner to a child of the age of four? Regardless of your statements, your areas of focus, and your emotional state. Please bear in mind that the subconscious mind can be likened to an uncontrollable genie that constantly impels us to manifest our desires. Consequently, it is important to reflect on what areas of focus occupy our thoughts. Are you currently prioritizing your well-being? Are you currently prioritizing the accumulation of wealth?

Are you implying that you are contented and enjoy a fulfilling romantic partnership, characterized by a deep affection for your spouse? Alternatively, are you indicating that you plan to foster a healthier relationship, emphasizing the current absence thereof?

Please consider the aforementioned seven distinct qualities of the subconscious mind that I have presented to you. Please bear in mind these traits whenever you are attempting to envision. The fundamental elucidation of the Law of Attraction can be characterized as follows - whatever thoughts or attention one directs their focus towards, that is precisely what becomes attracted to them. Hence, upon examining the aforementioned qualities inherent in the subconscious mind, it becomes apparent that the attributes of the subconscious align closely with those of the Law of Attraction. Wherever you direct your attention and cultivate a prevailing sentiment, that is precisely what will manifest within your reality. Take a moment to consider this. The manner in which you perceive and experience every aspect of life dictates your way of existence. It is inherent to your being, and you will consistently manifest more of your core essence.

A Concise Chronology of Creative Visualization

The utilization of creative visualization techniques and competencies has been employed and implemented over an extended period of time to foster the attainment of success in competitive sports. Over the past decade, the majority of athletes worldwide have adopted a mindset of considering themselves winners even prior to engaging in competition.

The individual known as DR serves as a testament to the transformative potential of creative visualization in one's life. Denis Whitely. I am confident that you are familiar with the account of an accomplished individual who asserts that the employment of creative visualization has played a pivotal role in shaping his present identity.

It is an indisputable fact that the practice of sports visualization has demonstrated its effectiveness over a significant span of time. This signifies that just as accomplished athletes employ the technique of creative visualization to envision their success, you have the ability to engage in these visualization practices as well, in order to shape yourself into the individual you have always aspired to become.

Benefits of Engaging in Creative Visualization

Upon surveying your surroundings or perusing online literature pertaining to creative visualization, you will encounter numerous captivating narratives of triumph and individuals who have effectively employed creative visualization to manifest favorable outcomes.

One might be curious as to how such occurrence comes about. The occurrence is such that one restricts their cognitive faculties and convictions, thereby confining their thought processes within a confined circumference. Once one becomes cognizant of the potent and transformative abilities inherent in creative visualization, it becomes imperative to strive towards harnessing its fullest capabilities in order to effect profound change in one's life.

It is important for you to recognize that you were destined to lead a fulfilling life, distinct from the burdens and challenges you encounter on a daily basis. The positive development is that you possess the means to achieve your aspirations. You possess boundless authority which you can utilize to revolutionize every aspect of your existence. If one desires increased happiness, it is paramount to engage in contemplation of additional joy, affluence, well-being, contentment, and achievement. These desirable outcomes can be effectively attained through the utilization of the transformative potential inherent in the practice of creative visualization.

The utilization of creative visualization is advisable for individuals at various intervals. If you still harbor doubts regarding its efficacy, allow me to elucidate four compelling justifications for incorporating creative visualization as a prominent component of your lifestyle.

Reason #1: You become the best version of your self

It is imperative that you acknowledge the correlation between your predicaments and the quality of life you currently experience, which can largely be attributed to your perceptions. For instance, when you engage in the act of envisioning becoming more compassionate, achieving success, attaining good health, and experiencing happiness, you transmit favorable cues to your subconscious mind.

Your subconscious mind assimilates and directs your energies in a manner that aligns with the achievement of your aspirations, ambitions, and objectives. Consequently, through the utilization of imaginative visualization, you will undoubtedly mold and construct your life in alignment with these objectives. This implies that your mental imagery correlates directly with your possession.

This fact alone constitutes ample justification for incorporating creative visualization into your daily routine as a customary activity, comparable to ordinary practices or habits like toothbrushing. Indeed, it is within your capacity to attain anything your heart desires in your lifetime. There are no dreams that are unattainable.

The rationale behind this is that there are no limitations to what you can imagine, and any concept you can envision holds potential through the faculty of creative visualization. Simply make a definitive choice at this very moment to construct your life in accordance with your exact desires.

Secondly, you experience an increased manifestation of synchronicity in your daily existence.

Through the consistent application of creative visualization on a daily basis, one can promptly realize or attain aspirations that have long been harbored. Through the application of imaginative visualization, significant opportunities will manifest. As an illustration, it is plausible that novel business concepts may begin to take shape in your mind, concepts that were hitherto unexplored or unimagined.

You may have the opportunity to engage with inspiring individuals who can instill motivation within you, as well as potentially gain a sudden burst of clarity in finding solutions to any challenges you are encountering or in achieving your objectives.

The practice of imaginative visualization can facilitate the identification of aspects that have eluded your attention, leading to the discovery of viable solutions. Additionally, it will aid in determining the appropriate steps for regaining control over one's life.

The third reason pertains to the revelation of one's higher calling or purpose.

Have you ever contemplated the notion of discovering a means by which to cease engaging in activities that are displeasing to you, and instead embarking upon the pursuit of your true calling? Maybe yes maybe no. Utilizing imaginative conceptualization is the most effective method to delineate the process of transitioning from your current state to one that is more deserving, while also outlining the necessary steps required to achieve this desired outcome.

The remarkable capability of visualization will provide you with discernment regarding the necessary actions to pursue your ambitious aspirations. Consequently, you will initiate behaving and moving in the direction aligned with your goals, ultimately resulting in the accomplishment of your objectives.

Fourthly, one experiences an increase in overall happiness.

By engaging in daily creative visualization, one can cultivate heightened levels of happiness, confidence, and mental resilience. The act of envisioning a life imbued with meaning, accomplishment, and an optimistic outlook brings about transformations in both one's physical presentation and the chemical makeup of the brain.

This phenomenon occurs due to a lack of differentiation between objective reality and the cognitive constructs already formed within your mind. In due time, you will begin to react in accordance with the state of your mindset, thus leading a life that you have envisioned even prior to its realization.

Rule 6: If an individual experiences persistent emotional distress, it is likely to result in physiological alterations over time.

The connection between the mind and body is indissoluble. Individuals afflicted with poor health and debilitating ailments frequently experience recurrent instances of the associated symptoms, until discernible physiological alterations can be detected.

A significant proportion of medical professionals acknowledge that over 70% of human ailments stem from emotional factors, rather than organic causes. The subliminal mind exerts a substantial influence on our corporeal state.

Frequently, addressing the emotional manifestation can lead to the resolution of a physical affliction. Positive thoughts and positive emotions give rise to constructive evolutionary transformations. By cultivating optimistic thoughts, one has the ability to generate affirmative emotions, ultimately resulting in the establishment of favorable physiological transformations within the body as time progresses.

Rule 7: The implementation of every suggestion leads to a diminished resistance towards subsequent suggestions.
The longer a mental trend persists without interruption, the more convenient it becomes to adhere to. As you engage in a given activity repeatedly, the neural connections associated with it are fortified and solidified, rendering them resistant to alteration or discontinuation.

Once a behavior becomes ingrained, it becomes increasingly effortless to adhere to and progressively challenging to relinquish. Hence, when engaging in autosuggestion or affirmation techniques, it is advisable to initially employ simple affirmations in order to yield positive outcomes. Incremental successes pave the path to a significant triumph.

Rule 8: In regards to the subconscious mind and its operations, an inverse relationship exists between the level of conscious exertion and the corresponding subconscious reaction.
One's endeavors to effectuate a modification in their everyday existence through deliberate exertion shall invariably prove futile. A reverse outcome will transpire wherein your attempts to alter your current state will solely serve to reinforce the habit or characteristic in question.

This substantiates the inefficacy of willpower. The concept of willpower implies that one is exerting effort towards a task or objective that they inherently lack enthusiasm or desire for. Take insomnia as an example: the more levels of effort one exerts in attempting to attain sleep, the more elusive sleep becomes.

The efficacy of visualization has been elucidated through an examination of the principles outlined within the eight rules of the mind, with particular emphasis on the first, second, and third rules.

The conscious mind exhibits a personalized nature and exercises selectivity, whereas the subconscious mind lacks individuation and operates in a non-discriminatory manner. The conscious mind can be seen as the outcome, whereas the subconscious mind can be perceived as the underlying catalyst. The conscious mind produces thoughts or concepts, which are then instilled within the subconscious mind. The subconscious mind assimilates thoughts or ideas, manifesting them into tangible reality. The subconscious mind never generates an idea or thought.

And by means of the intricate processes and mechanisms exclusive to the realm of the subconscious mind, these concepts materialized into tangible actuality. The mechanism of this creation is concealed within the depths of the subconscious mind. The subconscious mind transcends rationality and remains impervious to empirical evidence. It acknowledges a sentiment or emotional state as an indisputable reality. Drawing from this FACT, it imbues structure or contour to the sentiments or emotions. Hence, the process of manifestation commences with the inception of a desire, progresses with the conception of an idea, and culminates with the impetus to take action and yield a desired outcome.

The notion ingrained within the subliminal realm by means of emotional experience. When an emotionally charged idea, whether positive or negative, permeates and is embraced by the subconscious mind, it inevitably materializes in reality, regardless of its nature as either beneficial or detrimental. Consequently, an individual who fails to regulate their emotions will inadvertently implant negative ideologies into the depths of their subconscious, resulting in the consequences they experience.

Exercising emotional regulation does not entail restraining or repressing one's emotions. Exerting emotional regulation entails visualizing and experiencing constructive emotions conducive to personal ease and joy. It is crucial to regulate one's emotions. Do not perpetuate or prolong the experience of negative emotions within yourself. It is imperative that one refrains from succumbing to negative emotions, be they self-generated or influenced by external sources. This includes avoiding exposure to negative news, abstaining from watching television shows or movies with unfavorable content, and refraining from listening to songs that convey negativity.

Why? Due to this sentiment, irrespective of its origins or triggers, it is you who experiences it, rather than anyone else. Henceforth, any actions or thoughts, directed toward oneself or others, that engender adverse emotions or sentiments, should be evaded. Each emotion will generate a mark or marks within the depths of the subconscious, and if left uncounteracted by a more potent emotion, it shall invariably manifest itself in actuality. It is imperative to thoroughly analyze one's emotional state and sentiment, as one's perceived reality and existence are shaped by their emotional experiences.

The subconscious mind consistently brings forth the latent ideas or thoughts that have been ingrained within it without fault. Upon receiving the initial seed of an idea, the mind promptly initiates its operations, often employing mechanisms that elude recognition or conscious awareness, thereby materializing the notion into tangible existence. It is important to note that despite the subconscious mind dutifully manifesting the desires of the conscious mind, their dynamic does not resemble that of a master and servant. The subconscious mind is averse to being coerced. He exhibited a more favorable receptiveness towards persuasion as opposed to command or directive. Hence, the subconscious mind can be likened to a romantic partner rather than a subordinate.

The principle of visualization entails that new concepts or notions will become ingrained in your subconscious when you possess assurance and believe in their actualization or manifestation in the physical realm. Impression determines expression. The subconscious mind acknowledges and internalizes your emotions as truth or correctness, rather than your thoughts and beliefs. Therefore, your prevailing emotions dictate your perception of reality. Through the acquisition of this knowledge, you have the ability to construct your envisioned utopia.